Photography: How to Improve Your Technique

Photography
How to Improve Your Technique

By Catherine Noren

Photographs by the author

FRANKLIN WATTS, INC. • NEW YORK

1973

The photograph on p. 19 is
courtesy of James R. Smith.

Library of Congress Cataloging in Publication Data

Noren, Catherine.
   Photography: how to improve your technique.

   (A Concise guide)
   SUMMARY: Directions on choosing equipment and
film, using light, developing film, and numerous other
techniques that can improve photo-taking skills.
   Bibliography: p.
   1. Photography—Juvenile literature.
[1. Photography] I. Title.
TR149.N67   770.28   73-5687
ISBN 0-531-02640-X

Contents

Photography: How to Improve Your Technique

Introduction

When my best friend came back from her vacation in Europe, she was bubbling with excitement. She'd had a wonderful time, and she couldn't wait to show me her photographs of Italy, France, and Switzerland, to relive her vacation with me.

"There! That's me!" she said, pointing to some Roman ruins. I looked closely; in the middle of the ruins I saw a tiny, unrecognizable figure.

"Look at this Greek column, isn't it beautiful?" she exclaimed, handing me another print. The column was beautiful — what I could see of it. Its base started somewhere in the middle of the print, and its shaft disappeared off the top.

"That's the beach where we camped," she announced proudly. I looked and saw a gray blur.

Well, you get the idea. My friend had bought a camera especially for her trip to Europe. But she hadn't learned how to use it properly, and most of her photographs were still in her head.

Just as there is a language of words, there is also a language of photography; in fact, the word *photography*, which comes from the Greek, means "writing with light." Before you can write with words, you must know the letters of the alphabet; and before you can write with light, you need to know the elements of the photographic alphabet.

The purpose of this book is to help you learn the alphabet of photography — cameras, lenses, film, composition, what subjects to photograph and how best to photograph them, what happens in the darkroom.

Let's start with the "A" of photography — the camera.

1

Choosing Your Equipment

What Is a Camera?

A camera is a box with a piece of light-sensitive film in one side and a hole in the opposite side. The purpose of a camera is to let light strike the film and form an image on it.

Cameras range in price from $5 to $5,000; but all cameras, except the very simplest, have the following mechanisms in one form or another: a viewing system, a focusing device, a lens, a diaphragm, a shutter, a button for opening the shutter, and an advancing mechanism.

And all cameras, from the cheapest to the most expensive, work on the same general principle; they work the same way as our eyes work. Although we don't usually think of it this way, seeing is the most basic form of photography. Our eyes are cameras; they write with light on the brain. To understand how a camera "sees," let's compare its mechanisms to the mechanisms that enable our eyes to see.

The eye has two principal parts: in front it has a lens, which, like the lens of a camera, gathers light to form an image on the sensitive retina. The retina of the eye is comparable to the film in a camera: it records an image. You might say that the retina is like a piece of film on which the light-sensitive emulsion is continuously renewed.

In order to lessen the shock of changing light intensity, the eye — and the camera — has a diaphragm. The diaphragm of the eye works automatically, opening and closing according to the intensity of the light. Look at yourself in a mirror in a dimly

2

lit room; you'll notice that the pupils of your eyes are quite big. This is because they have automatically widened to let in more light. Now have a friend shine a flashlight on your face, and watch your pupils close down and become small in reaction to the bright light. The camera's diaphragm works the same way.

Our eyes focus automatically; a camera has a focusing device, usually a ring on the lens, which you adjust according to what you see in the viewing screen.

The camera shutter, a protective shield built into either the lens or the body of the camera, is like the eyelid; it protects the film from light. When you push the button to take a picture, the button causes the shutter to open and let light strike the sensitive film.

The other major mechanism on a camera is its advancing mechanism, which is used after you have taken a picture to bring a new, unexposed frame of film into place. The eye, of course, has no mechanism similar to the camera's advancing mechanism, as the images recorded on the brain are transitory, and the light-sensitive chemical on the retina is continuously renewing itself.

Kinds of Cameras

You wouldn't try to drive a Cadillac across the Sahara Desert; it would get stuck in the sand. The car for that kind of terrain would be a Land Rover. But if you're driving across the United States on a superhighway, a Cadillac would be fine; it's big and it's fast and it's comfortable. If you live in the city, where there is lots of traffic and very little parking space, a Volkswagen might be just the right car for you; it's small and easy to maneuver.

Just as you'd choose a car according to where you're going to be driving it, you'll want to choose the camera that's best suited for the kind of photographs you take.

Instamatics

Although the word *Instamatic* is actually a Kodak trade name, I shall use it here to refer to all brands of simple, instamatic-type cameras.

Instamatics are the least expensive and the easiest to operate of all cameras. You can buy one for around $10.

Instamatics use size 126 film, which comes in cartridges of twelve frames per cartridge. You load the film by simply dropping the cartridge in and snapping the camera shut. Most instamatic-type cameras do not have adjustable controls — that is, the mechanisms described earlier in this section are pre-set. This is both an advantage and a disadvantage. It's an advantage because there are no settings to fumble with. You just aim and shoot, and everything from about four feet away and farther will be in focus. The disadvantage of these nonadjustable and semiadjustable cameras is that you are limited in what you can shoot and where. On many of the instamatic-type cameras, the shutter speed is set, usually at about 1/50 of a second, so you can't photograph subjects that are in action. If you photograph a moving train, for instance, you will only get a blur. And because the diaphragm opening is also set, it's difficult to shoot in low light conditions. You must use a flash.

Polaroids

In the United States alone, amateur photographers snap about five billion photographs a year, and about one billion of these photographs are taken with polaroid cameras.

Unlike any other camera system now in existence, Polaroids give you instant photographs. Within ten minutes after pushing the button, you have the finished print in your hands. The

Above, an instamatic camera with nonadjustable controls
Below, the Polaroid. It produces instant photographs.

Polaroid process, invented by scientist Edwin Land, develops the negative and the print right inside the camera.

Polaroids range in price from $20 to $200. They are as easy to operate as the instamatics; their controls are pre-set. In addition to the regular mechanisms, they have a simple series of buttons and levers that you work to operate the print-developing system inside the camera and to release the finished print.

The major advantage of instant photography is that you can reshoot your photograph if you don't like what you got the first time. If photography is more than just a hobby for you, a Polaroid might be an excellent camera for you to own, because being able to see your picture immediately after you shoot it means that you can learn from your mistakes while they're still fresh in your memory.

35 Millimeter Cameras

There are two main types of 35 millimeter cameras — the rangefinder and the single-lens reflex, or SLR, as it is generally called. I have grouped them together, because they are more or less interchangeable in terms of the kinds of photography they are good for. Rangefinders and most SLRs are light, compact, and easily manageable cameras, ideal for shooting candid photos and fast-action events. They are more expensive than the instamatic types, ranging in price from $100 up. However they are more economical in terms of the film they use. They take size 135 film, which comes in cassettes of either 20 or 36 frames. Each frame is only 35 millimeters wide — about 1½ inches — and because it is so small, you can shoot a lot of frames quite inexpensively. A roll of 135-36 black-and-white film costs about a dollar. Instead of paying for enlargements of every frame you

Above, a 35 millimeter single-lens reflex
Below, a 35 millimeter rangefinder camera

7

shoot, it is possible to get a tiny print, the same size as the frame (35 mm), to look at. You can then decide whether you want to invest the money to have an enlargement made. These small prints are called contacts; the 20 or 36 contact prints for a roll of black-and-white film are printed side by side on a sheet of paper called a contact sheet.

Thirty-five millimeter cameras have adjustable controls and interchangeable lenses (see p. 10 for a discussion of lenses), which make them more versatile than the instamatic types. They have a focusing ring on the lens, a diaphragm that you can open up in low light or stop down in bright sun, and a variety of shutter speed settings. Their viewing system is a sort of peephole that you hold at eye level, and use more or less as an extension of your eye.

SLRs have more parts and are heavier and more complicated than rangefinders. They are also more delicate.

Some SLRs — most notably the Hasselblad, the camera that went to the moon — are built to take size 120 or 220 film. Size 120 film comes in rolls of 12 frames, 220 in rolls of 22 frames, and each frame measures $2\frac{1}{4}$ x $2\frac{1}{4}$ inches. This is an advantage, because the larger the negative, the sharper the enlargement will be. However, the $2\frac{1}{4}$ SLRs have the disadvantage of being much slower to handle, as their viewing system is one you look down into, as you hold the camera at waist level. They are also larger, heavier, and considerably more expensive than the eye-level SLRs. Generally speaking, they are best suited for studio work or for photographing still lifes, landscapes, and other stationary things.

Twin-Lens Reflex Cameras

The twin-lens reflex, as its name suggests, has two lenses, one stacked above the other. These cameras are similar to the SLRs

A twin-lens reflex

8

in that they also take size 120 film and that you hold them at waist level and look down into the viewing system.

Like the SLR, the twin-lens reflex uses a mirror to project the image onto the viewing screen. But the image you see is not the same image as the film will record, because the mirror mechanism is behind the upper lens, while the film plane is behind the lower lens. The advantage of this system is that the mirror remains fixed and does not have to be snapped out of the way of the film. This makes the twin-lens reflex both quieter to shoot with and less likely to break down.

The biggest problem with this system is the possibility of parallax error — an error in composition you could make by thinking that the image you will get is exactly the image you are seeing on the viewing screen. In fact, it will be only the bottom half of that image on the viewing screen, because the picture-taking lens is stacked below the viewing lens. There are some twin-lens reflexes that are built to automatically correct parallax in the camera.

Another major disadvantage of the twin-lens reflex is that while it does have adjustable controls, most models are not built to take interchangeable lenses. And its size, like that of the $2\frac{1}{4}$ SLRs, makes it better suited for studio work and still lifes than for candid photography.

About Lenses

When you look at an object, what your eye sees is not the object itself but an image of the object caused by light reflecting off it. The same is true when a camera "looks" at an object. But when light falls on an object, it does not reflect the image that we see. On the contrary, it bounces off and scatters all over the place. If we could see it in this way, what we would see would be a jumbled blur.

A lens is a light-gatherer. It gathers the scattering light particles and bends them toward each other until they converge to form the image that we see.

When a light ray strikes a piece of glass at an angle, it will bend. The scientific word for this property of light is refraction. So, when the scattering light rays hit a convex lens (the oval kind, thicker in the middle than at the edges), they reverse their direction, bend back toward each other until they meet, forming the image that we see. The point at which they meet is called the focal point, and it is at this focal point that the film is positioned in the camera, ready to record the image formed by the lens.

If the lens is very thick and very curved, the light rays will bend sharply because the angle at which they hit the lens is sharper. And because they bend sharply, they will meet only a short distance behind the lens, and produce a smaller image. A thin lens with less curvature will bend the light rays less, and the distance between the lens and the focal point will be greater, producing a larger image. This distance — the distance between the lens and the focal point — is called the focal length of the lens. It is measured in millimeters, and usually indicated on the rim of the lens. Lenses with short focal lengths are known as wide-angle lenses, because although they project smaller images, they take in a wide angle of vision. Lenses with long focal lengths are called telephoto lenses because they act like telescopes, bringing faraway objects close and magnifying them.

Lenses come in many different focal lengths — 28 mm, 35 mm, 50 mm, 90 mm, 105 mm, 135 mm, 200 mm, and longer. On most cameras, a normal lens — so-called because it is closest to the way our eyes see — has a focal length of about 50 mm.

I shot these three photos from the same distance, using three different lenses: a 35 mm, a 45 mm, and a 135 mm. With the 35 mm, you can see the whole car, plus a bit of its surroundings; with the 45 mm, you can see only part of the car; and with the 135 mm, all you can see is the door, with all its details visible and in sharp focus.

A final word about your equipment. As you continue to take photographs, your eye will become sharper, your seeing more sophisticated, and you will want to experiment with different kinds of photographs and new ways of seeing. That's fine. But be careful about buying equipment. Don't buy anything that you don't need. Many photographers make the mistake of acquiring too much equipment too soon. This can be a trap. An expensive camera or a fancy lens will not automatically produce a great photograph. The greatness of a photograph can be determined only by you, by what you see. Your eyes are your most important piece of photographic equipment.

I shot the first of these pictures with a 35-millimeter lens, the second with a 45-millimeter lens, and the third with a 135-millimeter lens.

How to Get What You See

I went to the zoo with my camera. The seals were the main attraction that day. They were giving a terrific performance, splashing and diving and playing tag. I shot frame after frame, and the one I was really anxious to see was the one of them whispering to each other. But when I saw the print, I was so disappointed! There they were, sharing their secret just as I had seen them — but I had included the bars of their cage in the frame, and the black bars cutting through their bodies ruined the illusion of sweetness and freedom.

It would have been a simple matter to place my camera between the bars to eliminate them from my photograph. But I didn't stop to think, I didn't look carefully enough, and so I lost what might have been a marvelous photograph.

Every photograph you plan to take brings its own set of problems with it, and for almost every photographic problem, there is a solution. Often the solution is as simple as moving yourself and your camera, or your subject.

Focusing for Best Effect

The first and most important thing to be aware of is focus. Cameras with adjustable controls have a focusing ring. (Nonadjustable cameras generally do not have a focusing ring.) You gauge focus by measuring the distance between your camera and your subject.

I should have placed my camera between the bars to eliminate them from the photograph.

14

You will almost always want the main subject of your photograph to be in sharp focus, but what about focus in the rest of your photograph?

Say you want to take a picture of your friend standing in front of her house. If you shoot both your friend and her house in sharp focus, you will probably get a confusing photograph — is it a photograph of your friend, or is it a photograph of your friend's house with your friend standing in front of it? But you do want a suggestion of the house, because it says something about your friend. So a soft-focus background is the solution to this problem. You'll see just enough of the house to recognize it, without having it interfere with the portrait of your friend.

The area in a photograph that is in sharp focus is called depth of field, and the mechanism that determines depth of field is the diaphragm. When the diaphragm is wide open — on most adjustable cameras, the widest opening is either f. 2 or f. 2.8 — the object you are focusing on will be sharp, but everything in front and behind it will be out of focus. The more you stop the diaphragm down — that is, close it — the greater the depth of field. In other words, more of the area in front of your subject and behind it will come into sharp focus. It's the same principle as squinting your eyes to see better: you don't let as much light in, but you can see farther.

When you are shooting in low light conditions you may have to keep the diaphragm wide open and sacrifice depth of field. In this instance, your choice will be dictated by necessity.

The other mechanism for controlling the light that strikes the film is the shutter speed. The shutter speed on different

The out-of-focus background gives
a feeling of activity to the
photograph without distracting
from its main subject, the girl.

17

cameras ranges from 1/2000 of a second to indefinite time exposures where you keep the shutter open as long as you want — hours, if need be. Set at 1/1000 of a second, the shutter opens for 1/1000 of a second and the film is exposed to light for 1/1000 of a second. At 1/60 of a second the film is exposed to light for 1/60 of a second.

Fast shutter speeds are used for stopping action. If you're photographing a horse galloping across a field and you want the horse to be in sharp focus, use a fast shutter speed, say 1/250, which is fast enough to stop most movement.

Fast shutter speeds are also good for very bright days when a slower shutter speed will overexpose the film.

Slow shutter speeds are used for photographing things that don't move. If something you're shooting moves while the shutter is open, it will appear blurred in the photograph. For photographing these still things, use a slow shutter speed and stop the diaphragm down. (The focus of most lenses is sharpest at f. 8 and f. 11.) About the slowest shutter speed at which you can hand-hold a camera is 1/60. For shutter speeds slower than 1/60, place the camera on a support — for example, a table, a box, a rock, or a tripod.

Slow shutter speeds can also be used to accentuate motion. Let's go back to that galloping horse for a minute. Try photographing it now at 1/125 or 1/60. You will get a blurred but recognizable horse, and often that kind of blurriness will give the feeling of movement, and be very effective.

Slow shutter speeds are also useful on dark days when you want to let as much light as possible onto the film.

Photographer James R. Smith
moved his camera with the galloping horse
and let the background blur to
give a feeling of the horse's speed.

Time exposures are good for photographing at night. You can leave the shutter open for as long as you want, and the small amount of available light will very slowly record an image on the film.

Composition

Composition is a word constantly used in connection with photography, but its exact meaning is often elusive. Briefly, composition is the way the elements in a photograph are arranged in relation to each other within the frame.

Let's consider each of these elements separately.

First, a good photograph needs a main point of interest. It's usually the subject of the photograph: who or what the photograph is about. A photograph without a main point of interest is confusing. Your eye doesn't know where to look first, and your brain doesn't know what the photograph is about.

Balance is another important element of composition. But balance doesn't mean that you should always center your subject. You can often create a more dramatic photograph by placing your subject to one side or above or below the center of the frame. Place another, less important, element in an opposite part of the frame to balance the subject. This will lead your eye from the less important to the more important element.

These two photographs illustrate two different principles of

Above, centering your subject is a simple and effective way of creating balance. Below, another way to create balance is to place different elements in different parts of the frame. Here, the main subject — the boy — is above center and to the left, and the balance is created by his own reflection, and the reflections of the buildings.

21

balance. Each is arranged in such a way as to make the most effective balance for its subject matter.

Think about distance and angle before you shoot. Should you photograph your subject head-on, or move to one side? Should you do a profile or front view? Should you shoot from above your subject, looking down, or from below, looking up? These are decisions only you can make, and you should base your decisions on what you want your photograph to say.

I took one of these photographs at a person's eye level and the other at the dog's eye level. Which is more effective? Why?

If you stand between a pair of railroad tracks and look down the line, you'll see that the tracks appear to meet, to converge, as they reach the horizon. They are not really converging, of course. Parallel lines never meet. What you are seeing is an illusion caused by perspective. Another illusion caused by perspective is to make faraway objects seem smaller than ones that are nearer. You can use these illusions of perspective to create a feeling of space in your photographs. Experiment with using lines — like a fence, or the line down the middle of a road, for example — that lead away from your camera to a faraway object to create a three-dimensional effect. When you look at your photograph, your eyes will seem to travel deep into it, even though it's only a piece of paper!

Be aware of the shapes of things, and contrast them to emphasize their differences. Photograph a round vase on a square table or a round baby playing with square building blocks. And do the opposite, too: photograph the same round vase full of round roses on a round table. Different elements that repeat the same shape or form will give your photograph a feeling of flow

One of these photographs is taken from a person's eye level, the other from the dog's. Which works better?

and rhythm as each element leads your eye smoothly to the next. Experiment with contrasting and similar textures, contrasting and similar colors.

As you look through the viewfinder of your camera, try to be aware of everything that appears in the frame. If you see something in your viewfinder that you don't want in your photograph, the time to get rid of it is before you push the button. You can almost always do this by moving either the object or your camera. The practice is known as cropping in the camera — visualizing how your photograph will look before you actually shoot it. (Later on, in the section on printing, you'll learn how to crop in the darkroom, but this isn't a good habit to get into and should be done only when absolutely necessary.) So look carefully before you push the button.

Despite these many elements that are the ingredients of a photograph, there is probably only one hard-and-fast rule concerning composition: keep it simple! The photograph you take is a statement about how you perceive the subject you are photographing, and the simpler you keep it, the more clearly your statement will be understood. So remember to include in your photograph only those elements that are part of your statement. If in doubt, leave it out.

Light

As a photographer, light is your most basic and important tool, and how you use it is vitally important to your photographs. This section on light is divided into two parts: the first is about

Above, parallel lines give the illusion of converging as they near the horizon. This is an illusion created by perspective. Below, repeating similar shapes and movements can create a harmonious — and sometimes funny — composition.

25

correct exposure; the second contains ideas about using light creatively.

Correct Exposure

Correct exposure is the amount of light that must strike the film in order for it to faithfully record the image.

If you shoot without enough light, your photograph will be underexposed, too dark — and you won't be able to see the details. If you let too much light strike the film, your photograph will be overexposed, too light — and you won't be able to see the details.

As you learned earlier, the camera's two mechanisms for controlling the amount of light striking the film are f. stops (diaphragm apertures) and shutter speeds. To illustrate how these mechanisms can work together, let's compare exposing a photograph to running a bath.

The water running into the tub would be equal to the light falling on the film, and a full bathtub would equal correct exposure. If you turn the faucet on wide, the tub will fill up quickly — say, in five minutes. This would be the equivalent of opening the diaphragm all the way and using a fast shutter speed. On the other hand, if you turn the faucet only halfway on, the tub will take twice as long to fill up, ten minutes. This would be the equivalent of stopping the diaphragm down halfway — say to f. 8 — and selecting a slower shutter speed to make sure you let in enough light.

How do you decide whether to open the diaphragm and use a fast shutter speed, or to stop down the diaphragm and use a slower shutter speed?

You have already learned how these controls affect focus and depth of field and how they can be used to stop action or accentuate it. These factors, plus the light conditions you are shooting in, will help you determine the most effective combination.

A light meter is a device specifically designed to "read" light and give you the correct exposure information. Some light meters are built into the camera, others are separate instruments that you hold in your hand.

Although it is not within the scope of this book to go into detail about light meters (if you have one or buy one, be sure you understand the instructions provided with it), there is one important piece of information that you should know about exposing film correctly.

Black-and-white film has a greater latitude for overexposure than underexposure, so it is better to overexpose than underexpose. When you take a light reading, point your meter at the darkest object that you'll want to see detail in. Say you are photographing a brown cat and a white cat sleeping in the same chair. If you aim your meter toward both cats, the meter will average the light reflecting off them and give you a reading somewhere in the middle, and this average reading will cause you to lose some of the detail in the brown cat. To compensate for this, take your reading from the brown cat only. That way you'll be sure to get all the detail your eye has seen, and you'll also be able, in the darkroom, to burn in the areas on the white cat that are too light. (See p. 49 for information about burning in.) If you can't get close enough to the black horse to take a proper reading, take your reading from an object near you that has the same tone — your shoes, for instance — and the same amount of illumination falling on it.

When you are shooting color film, however, it is better to lean toward underexposing. An overexposed color print or transparency looks washed out and flat, but a half a stop underexposure will make your colors deep and rich.

27

Above left, with the light coming from one side; above right, with the light coming from above; left center, with the light coming from behind; right center, with the light coming from beneath; left, with the light coming from directly in front.

Using Light Creatively

For this experiment you will need a patient friend and a movable light source — say, a light bulb on an extension cord. Walk slowly around your friend, aiming the light toward his or her face. First aim it at one side of the face, then directly in front; hold the light above the head, aiming it down, then beneath the chin, then behind the head. You will see that from each position, the light creates an entirely different mood.

With the light coming from one side, your friend's face looks cut in half; one side is well-lit, the other is in deep shadow. Light coming from directly above creates deep shadows under the eyes, nose, and chin. Light coming from behind creates a silhouette effect; the face will be in shadow, and the person will seem to be wearing a halo. With the light held below the chin, your friend will have an "evil look," like Boris Karloff. Aimed full face, the light will be even, but this tends to flatten features.

There's an old photographic rule that says: "Shoot with the sun at your back." While this is not a bad rule to follow, this experiment demonstrates that it is also a good rule to break, for interesting and dramatic effects.

For instance, I shot the hungry camel on the next page with my camera aimed directly into the sun. The sunspots have the effect of emphasizing his hump and his unique camel qualities.

Photograph the same scene — say, a landscape — at different times of day: early in the morning, at noon, and at sunset. You will have three very different photographs. Shoot outdoor scenes on hazy days, on cloudy days, on foggy days. Notice how the nature of the light affects the mood of your photograph. Take portraits of your friends outdoors. If it's a bright day, choose a shadowed area. Hazy sunlight has a soft and flattering effect. Shoot in the late afternoon, when the sun is low over the horizon. The long shadows cast can contribute dramatic elements to your composition.

29

So far, this discussion of light has been limited to available light — a photographic term referring to light that is already there, and available. Available light can be either daylight or artificial light. But you need not be limited to shooting by available light. There are a variety of supplementary light sources you can use if you don't have sufficient available light.

Flashbulbs and flashcubes are popular and effective supplementary light sources. They are easy to use; you need only follow the instructions that come with your camera to get a well-exposed photograph, and you can use them in any low-light situation — in the dark, at dusk, or in a dimly lit room.

Electronic flash — also called a speedlight — works on a slightly different principle than flashbulbs and flashcubes, and in many ways it is more convenient because there are no bulbs to change. It is a separate unit that may either be fastened to your camera or held separately. Its power comes from electricity stored within the unit. The electricity comes from either a wall outlet from which the unit has been charged, or from batteries in the unit itself. After the light has been used, the speedlight will recharge, or recycle, itself in a matter of seconds, and be ready for the next shot.

For a photographer, light is a complex subject. The best way that you can learn is to experiment. Don't be afraid to try new ways of using light. You learn as much from what doesn't work as from what does. And it's exciting, too.

How to Use the Film You Choose

Film is transparent acetate coated on one side with an emulsion. When light strikes the emulsion, it reacts chemically to form an image. Although the emulsion on all black-and-white film is

Hungry camel, with sun spots

basically the same, the thickness of the emulsion layer differs in different types of film. Generally speaking, the thicker the emulsion, the faster the film reacts to light. In other words, film with a thick layer of emulsion needs less light for correct exposure than does film with a thin layer. Thick-emulsion films are called fast films; thin-emulsion films are slow films.

The speed of a film is indicated by a number, written on the film package, called the ASA number (for American Standards Association, which devised this system of measurement). And, if you own a light meter, you'll notice that it has an ASA indicator. Before you take a light reading, be sure to set the indicator at the ASA number of the film you're shooting, in order to get exposure information that is correct for that film.

Black-and-White Films

There are a variety of black-and-white films on the market, with speeds ranging from 25 ASA to 1000 ASA. If you are shooting with an instamatic, you'll use Verichrome Pan, as it's the only kind of film made for cartridge-loading cameras. Verichrome Pan, or VP, has a film speed of 125 ASA, making it a medium-slow film, best suited for shooting outdoors or in bright artificial light. VP is also available in sizes 135 and 120.

The other two most popular types of black-and-white film are Plus-X, which is also rated at 125 ASA, and Tri-X, which has a speed of 400 ASA. If you compare a photograph shot with VP or Plus-X to one shot with Tri-X, you'll notice that the Tri-X print is slightly grainier than the other. Grain in a photograph is the thousands and thousands of tiny dots that make up the image. You have to look closely to pick out grain with your naked eye, but it's clearly visible through a magnifying glass.

I would recommend Tri-X. It's more versatile than the others because, being a fast film, you can use it in a greater variety of light conditions (since overexposure, if you remember, is not a serious problem with black-and-white film).

Color Films

Generally speaking, color film is slower than black-and-white, with ratings ranging from 16 ASA to 164 ASA. (If you're shooting color in low light, you'll need your flash.)

Correct exposure is more important with color than black-and-white, because color film has less margin for error. As I mentioned earlier, it's better to underexpose color than to overexpose it, although don't underexpose more than one f. stop or shutter speed setting.

Color films come in two types: negative and reversal. Color negative is similar to black-and-white negative in that the film, when processed, becomes a negative from which you can then have prints made.

Color reversal film has no negative; the film is processed directly into a positive image, called a transparency. Because transparencies are so small, the best way to see them properly is to project them onto the wall or onto a screen with a viewer. You can also have large prints made from transparencies. When buying color film, if you see "-chrome" tacked onto the end of the name of the film (such as Kodakchrome or Ektachrome) you know that it's color reversal. The word "color" (such as Kodacolor) indicates color negative.

There is one kind of color film made specifically for use in natural light, and a second kind that is color-balanced for artificial, or tungsten, light. The color film designed for use in natural light is called Type A, and has the letter A next to the film size on the package. Color film balanced for artificial light is called Type B, and has the letter B next to the film size. If you shoot Type A film by artificial light, your photograph or transparency will have a brownish-yellow cast; if you shoot Type B film out-doors, it will have a bluish cast.

Strange as it may seem, black-and-white photographs more closely resemble what our eyes see than do color photographs. Color film doesn't render the same colors that our eyes see — just look at any color print, and you'll see what I mean. For this reason, it can sometimes interfere with the statement of your photograph. Black-and-white, on the other hand, contains a great variety of tones, ranging from white-white through medium gray to the blackest black. These tones are easily translated by our eyes into the gradations of color that our eyes see. I'm not say-ing that black-and-white is better, but, believe it or not, it is often truer.

What to Photograph

There are twenty-four hours in every day, and for about sixteen hours of those twenty-four, your eyes are open and you are seeing. Every day a whole panorama of scenes passes before your eyes. People, animals, events, machines — what you see every day is endless.

Of this whole world of sixteen hours of seeing a day, how on earth do you decide what to photograph? What is it that makes one thing more meaningful than another, meaningful enough to take a photograph, a permanent image that you'll want to look at again and again?

Amazing as it seems, *you never see the same thing in the same way twice.* You may see the refrigerator in your kitchen fifteen or twenty times every day, but each time you look at it, you see it in a slightly different way. One time there might be a dish on top of it; then the dish will be gone; then the light in the kitchen may be on; then you might be standing beside it, so you only see its profile; then the door might be open; then the afternoon sun might be shining on it.

I don't suppose you want to photograph your refrigerator, but if you did, how would you photograph it? What does it mean to you? To me a refrigerator means food, so I would shoot it with the door open, showing the food inside. But if I lived in a tropical jungle, the most important thing about that refrigerator would probably be its coldness. So I might photograph the freezer compartment.

Back to the original question: what should you photograph?

Photograph something that you've never seen before. If you're going on a vacation, you will certainly want to photograph the places, people, and sights you see, as my friend did (remember her European vacation?). Your photographs will help you relive the pleasure of your trip and keep the memory of it fresh in your mind. And later, when you look at your photographs, you will learn more about the places where you have been and the people you met. Photographs often contain surprising secrets, which you can learn if you look at them again and again, and think hard about what they are telling you.

Photograph what you might never see again. The panda bears in the Washington Zoo (the only two in the United States); your great-uncle who came to visit from Russia; a rare spider in the garden or a hummingbird flying backwards; television coverage of a historical event (you can photograph the television screen and have it to show to your grandchildren someday!).

Photograph familiar subjects in a way that you've never seen them before. Sometimes a part of something can stand for the whole thing and be more original and interesting. Instead of photographing a baby and his mother, shoot just the baby's hands holding onto his mother's hands — that will tell the whole story about babies and mothers. A single flower instead of a whole vaseful; graffiti on a wall instead of the whole wall; a window with a curtain blowing instead of the whole house.

Photograph familiar subjects the way you remember them best. My friend Booker loves to play baseball; I hardly ever see him without a ball or a catcher's mitt or both. I can't think of Booker without thinking of a home run. One day I asked him to let me take his picture. He said okay, he'd pose for me.

I wasn't too happy. So one day, when he didn't even know I was around, I took his picture. I think that is the one that I'll keep.

Often a single detail can tell a whole story, as in this photograph.

Booker posing for his picture

Booker, when he isn't posing

Try to capture emotion in your photographs: haste — someone running for a bus; waste — an overflowing litter basket; taste — your brother (or sister, or mother, or father) biting into a piece of cake; humor — a circus clown doing his thing; secrets — two girls whispering and giggling together; togetherness — four people in a phone booth; wintertime — a deserted park bench in the snow.

Here are some other ideas; I'm sure you can think of interesting ways to photograph them: interesting faces; signs; food; shadows and patterns; water; weddings; school events; sports; famous people; news events; feeding time at the zoo; street scenes; historical places and buildings; statues; famous paintings and sculptures; concerts; happenings; the changing surf; sights at dawn and at dusk; a small child's first roller coaster ride; parades; state fairs; a small child with a special toy; store windows with interesting displays; model sailboats on a pond; big sailboats on the ocean; an apple orchard in autumn; a barnyard in winter; a cactus blooming in the desert.

The world is full of photographs, just look around you. . . .

In the Dark

These are the three activities that happen in the darkroom: your exposed film is processed to produce a permanent negative image, one in which the tones are reversed, so that the light tones appear dark and the dark tones appear light. The negative can then be used to make both prints and enlargements. In this section, I shall talk about processing and printing black-and-white film. Color is processed by a different and considerably more complex method.

Developing Film into Negative

Developing film into negative is done in four major steps. First the film is immersed in a chemical solution called a developer, which reacts with the light-exposed emulsion of the film to form an image. When the image has formed on the film, the film is immersed in a solution of acetic acid, which stops the developing process, so that the film will not be overdeveloped. Then it is immersed in another bath known as fixer, or hypo, which makes the image permanent by washing away unused chemicals, hardening the emulsion and keeping the image from fading. Finally, the negative is thoroughly washed to remove all left-over traces of chemicals and then dried.

You don't need an actual darkroom to process film; you can do it in any room that you can make completely light-tight for the time it takes you to load the film into the developing tank.

In addition to a light-tight room, you'll need the following equipment, which you can buy in the darkroom department of any camera-supply store:

1. A measuring cup or darkroom graduate.
2. A film developing tank. This can be either plastic or

stainless steel; both kinds come with a reel that fits inside, on which to load your film.

3. Developer. There are a number of different kinds of developer on the market; I recommend Kodak D-76. It comes in powder form, which you mix with water according to the instructions on the can.

4. Indicator Stop Bath, which is used to stop the action of the developer. You dilute it with water according to the instructions on the bottle.

5. Fixer, also called hypo. Like the developers, there are a variety of fixers on the market. I recommend Kodafix. It comes pre-mixed and you dilute it with water according to the instructions.

6. Photo-Flo. After washing the negative, this solution is used to remove any residual water stains. Dilute it with water according to the instructions.

7. Three 16-ounce containers.

8. A darkroom thermometer for measuring the temperature of your chemicals.

9. A clock or watch with a second hand.

10. A squeegee or a sponge.

11. Two film clips — clothespins will do just as well.

12. Access to running water.

When you've gotten all this equipment, you're ready to start. The first step is to mix your chemicals — the developer, stop bath, and fixer — with water according to the instructions that accompany them. Mix 16 ounces of each, and put each in one of the containers. The temperature of your chemicals is important. Recommended developing times are based on a traditional darkroom temperature of 68 degrees. If your chemical solutions are too warm, the film will overdevelop, and become too dark, and if your chemicals are too cold, the opposite will happen.

After you've mixed them, if you find that the chemicals are

either too warm or too cold, place the containers in a sink of cold or hot running water until they're the right temperature. And as you mix the chemicals, be sure to rinse out your measuring cup after each use, so the different chemicals won't contaminate each other.

Now take your film, the film tank and reel, and yourself into your "dark" room, and turn out the lights. In *total darkness*, open up the film. Size 126 cartridges can be twisted open; 35 mm cassettes can be opened with a bottle opener. Load the film onto the reel according to the instructions that come with the tank. (It's a good idea to practice this first in the light with an old roll of film so that your hands will be quite sure of what they're doing when your eyes can't help.) A word of warning: if you're using a plastic reel, be sure that your hands, the film, and the reel are all absolutely dry. If there's any moisture on them, the film will become sticky, and you won't be able to get it onto the reel.

After you've finished loading the film, put the reel into the tank and screw the cover on tightly. It has a light-tight hole in the top, through which you pour the chemicals. Now you can turn on the light.

Pour the developer into the tank and leave it there for the developing time recommended on the can for the kind of film you're using. For five seconds out of every thirty, gently agitate the tank with a circular motion, to make sure that the developer covers the film evenly. At the end of the developing time, pour the developer out of the tank and back into its container.

Now pour in the stop bath. Leave it in for about fifteen seconds, agitating gently, then pour it out and back into its container.

Pour in the fixer, and agitate as you did the developer. Leave it in for the time recommended on the package or bottle. Then pour it out.

Now the film has been fixed and the image made permanent, you can take the cover off the film tank. Place the open tank with the reel in it under cool running water, letting the film wash for at least half an hour. Then immerse the film for fifteen or twenty seconds in the Photo-Flo.

Unwind the film from the reel, place a clothespin on one end (be careful to clip it on the very end of the film so as not to damage your first frame), hang it up, and gently wipe the film down with the squeegee or sponge. Hang the film up to dry in a dust-free place. To keep it from curling, weight the bottom of the film with the other clothespin or film clip.

When the film is dry (you should count on about six hours' drying time), cut it into strips of from four to six frames, and store the strips from each roll together in a glassine envelope, which you can also buy in a camera-supply store.

Evaluate your negative. A normal negative is one in which the highlight and shadow (dark and light) areas are distributed evenly, and you can see the detail in both.

A thin negative looks the way its name implies. It is very light, almost transparent, because the emulsion has been washed away during the developing process. A thin negative comes from underexposure. When too little light strikes the film, the chemicals will wash away the areas of emulsion that have not received any or enough light, leaving just the transparent acetate.

A dense negative, one that is too dark, is caused by overexposing. If too much light has struck the film, too little of the emulsion will be washed away in the developing process.

Above, a normal, properly exposed negative
Center, a thin, underexposed negative
Below, a dense, overexposed negative

44

Making Prints

When you make a print, or enlargement, you force light through the negative onto a piece of light-sensitized paper, which is similar to light-sensitized film in that it is coated on one side with a light-sensitive emulsion. Because the dark areas of a negative will let the least light through and the light areas will let the most light through, the response of photographic printing paper is the opposite of that of film: the areas that appear light on the negative will be dark on the positive — the print — and vice-versa. This will reverse the tones of the image to their natural state. Except for this basic reversal, the print-making process is similar to processing film.

First, light is forced through the negative and onto the paper. This is done with an enlarger, the most important piece of darkroom equipment. The exposed paper is immersed in developer, where the image becomes visible; then in stop bath; then in fixer, to wash away left-over chemicals and make the image permanent. Then the print is washed and dried.

You'll need this equipment for making prints:

1. An enlarger with a negative carrier.
2. An easel to hold the printing paper.
3. A darkroom. It doesn't have to be as light-tight as the room in which you load film, because paper is not quite as sensitive to light as film is.
4. A safelight.
5. Printing paper (for an explanation of what kind to buy, see p. 51).
6. Four trays, each large enough to hold the printing paper.
7. Print developer. This is slightly different from film developer. I recommend Kodak Dektol.
8. Indicator Stop Bath.
9. Fixer. You can use Kodafix for printing, also. However,

the ratio of water to fixer is different than for film processing. Read the instructions.

10. A darkroom timer or a clock with a second hand.

11. Two pairs of tongs: one for moving the print from the developer to the stop bath, the other for moving it from the stop bath to the fixer.

12. Access to running water.

13. A blotter roll or blotter pad to dry your prints.

Your first step is to mix the chemicals. This time you'll put them in trays instead of containers. Mix developer, stop bath, and fixer according to the instructions given for making prints. Arrange the trays in this order: developer, stop bath, fixer, and then a tray with water to wash the prints.

You're ready to start printing. Slip your negative into the negative carrier, holding it by the edges to avoid getting finger-prints on the image, which might show up on the print. Put the negative in the carrier with its emulsion side, the dull side, down, facing the easel. Turn the overhead light off and the safe-light on. Open the diaphragm of the enlarger lens all the way, and turn the enlarger light on. The image of your negative will be projected onto the easel. By racking the enlarger head up or down, make your image larger or smaller until the whole image appears in the frame of the easel.

Adjust the focusing device on the enlarger until the image on the easel is as sharp as possible. Now stop down the dia-phragm of the lens. An enlarger lens is sharpest three stops down, which is usually f. 8 or f. 11.

The next thing to do is to make a test strip to find the right exposure for your negative. Time of exposure in an enlarger, which is comparable to the shutter speed on your camera, can be anywhere from one second to one minute or longer. For a nor-mal negative, it's usually between five and twenty seconds.

Turn the enlarger light off, and set the timer at five seconds. Take half a piece of printing paper and lay it on the easel emulsion side, the shiny side, up. Cover two-thirds of the paper with a piece of cardboard. Turn on the enlarger light, and expose the uncovered portion for five seconds. When the light goes off, uncover another third of the paper and expose the uncovered two-thirds for another five seconds. Then uncover the rest of your test strip, and expose the whole strip for five more seconds. Now you have exposed the first section for fifteen seconds, the second section for ten seconds, and the third section for five seconds.

Slide your test strip into the devoloper tray and leave it there for about a minute and a half, gently rocking the tray to make sure the developer covers the paper evenly. Then put it in the stop bath for about fifteen seconds, and then into the fixer. When it is completely immersed in the fixer, you can turn on the overhead light.

Which exposure time has given you the truest and most pleasing image? It may be five, ten, or fifteen seconds; or somewhere in between, or more or less than one of those times.

After you have decided, you're ready to make a print. Go back to the enlarger, set the timer, and turn off the overhead light. Now take out a whole sheet of printing paper, and expose and process it the same way you did the test strip. This time, leave it in the fixer for five to ten minutes (although it's all right to turn on the overhead light when you're sure it's fully immersed). When the print has been properly fixed, put it in the water to wash. As you will need to wash it under running water, you can either buy a tray siphon with a hose that attaches to a faucet, or else you can set the tray in the sink or bathtub under the running water. Your print should wash for at least an hour.

After washing, place it, picture-side toward the linen surface, in your blotter to dry.

Now you have a finished print, just like the image you saw, not so long ago, in your viewfinder.

In the section on composition (p. 21), I mentioned cropping in the darkroom. Sometimes, instead of enlarging the entire frame of a negative, you might want to print only a part of it. To crop or eliminate an unwanted section of your negative, rack the enlarger head up on its arm until only the part of the negative that you want appears within the frame of the easel.

There are some other things you can do to control your image. If you have a negative that is not evenly exposed, that has one area that is too thin or too dense, you can darken or lighten just that area without affecting or changing the over-all exposure time.

An area that is too thin will appear too dark on your print. To give the rest of your negative the proper exposure without letting that one section go too dark, you can hold back, or dodge, that section. This is done with a device appropriately called a dodger. You can buy a dodger in a camera-supply store, or you can make your own. Cut a circle of black cardboard a little larger than a quarter, and tape it onto a piece of stiff wire about sixteen inches long.

Estimate how much time your thin area will need for proper exposure, and after that much time has elapsed on the enlarger, hold the circle over the area to protect it from the enlarger light. Move the dodger in small circles while you're holding back, otherwise its outline, as well as the outline of the wire, will be visible on the print.

If there's a section of your negative that's too dark, the image on your print will be too light. To increase exposure time for that area, you can burn in. Take a piece of cardboard considerably larger than your print paper, and cut out a small circle somewhere near its center. Now, expose your print nor-

49

mally. Then, holding the circle above the area that needs more exposure, turn the enlarger on again and let the light shine through the hole. Be sure to keep the rest of the print paper covered by the cardboard. Again, move the cardboard in small circles while you're burning in.

Another way you control your image is by the enlarging paper you use. Enlarging papers come in six different grades, numbered 1 through 6, and each grade has a slightly different emulsion. Number 1 paper will give you a print with tones that range from light gray to dark gray, and is called a soft-contrast paper. The higher the grade, the more contrasty the paper. On number 6, the most contrasty paper, many of the middle tones, the gray tones, will have dropped out, and the print will be more or less just black and white.

If you have a very contrasty negative — one that has very dark and very light areas but almost no middle tones — you would print it on soft-contrast paper to bring out whatever middle tones there are and to soften the harsh blacks and whites. A flat negative, one with little or no very dark or very light areas, will show a richer black and more brilliant white if printed on a high-contrast paper. A normal negative, one with a full range of tones, will usually print well on number 2 paper.

If you don't do much printing, you may not want to stock six different boxes of enlarging paper. An alternative is to buy one box of variable contrast paper. This paper comes in only one grade, and you vary its contrast by exposing it through a special set of filters. With a number 1 filter, the paper's contrast equals that of number 1 paper, and so forth.

The first photograph is
the full frame of the negative;
the second, a section of
that negative, cropped and enlarged.

51

Making Contacts

The process of making contact prints is essentially the same as making enlargements, with one exception. Instead of using the enlarger to blow up a single frame, you lay all the strips of negative from a roll of film side by side on one sheet of printing paper. (It's called a contact sheet because the paper is printed by actual contact with the negative.)

You don't need an enlarger for making contact sheets; you can expose them to a regular 100-watt frosted light bulb. Nor do you actually need a darkroom, although you will need a safelight, as well as the trays of chemicals you use for making prints.

In the dark, lay the printing paper emulsion-side up, and on top of it your strips of negative, emulsion-side down, side by side on the paper. Place the sheet of glass over them. The light bulb should be about four feet above the paper and the negatives. Now turn on the light, leave it on for about fifteen seconds, then turn it off again. Develop the paper the same way you would develop a regular print (using the safelight), and wash and dry it the same way. Now you can examine these tiny positives of all the film you shot, and pick the best ones to blow up into regular prints.

A Final Word

Photography is both an art and a science, and this is one of the things that makes it so fascinating. To be a skillful darkroom technician often requires a kind of scientific thinking and mathematical precision. But the results of this thinking and precision are finally measured in terms of their artistic value and pleasing effect. And the world of cameras and films — f. stops, shutter speeds, focal lengths, Tri-X, ASA numbers, grain — is essentially a scientific world. But knowing how to use that knowledge to photograph what you see in just the way you see it is an art.

In today's world of instant photographs, the art and science of photography can be as simple or as complicated as you want it to be. But whether you use an Instamatic or a Nikon, whether you have your prints processed for you or have your own elaborate darkroom set-up, the most important thing about photography is that you enjoy it.

Glossary

Advancing Mechanism: Camera mechanism used to bring a new, unexposed frame of film into place and ready to shoot.

ASA Number: Number that indicates the speed of the film.

Available Light: Natural or artificial light that is already there when you arrive on the scene.

Burning In: When making an enlargement, increasing exposure time for one small area of a negative.

Color Negative: Type of color film that is processed into negative, from which prints can be made.

Color Reversal: Type of color film that is processed into positive transparencies.

Composition: The way the elements in a photograph are arranged in relation to each other within the frame.

Contrast: Difference between the lightest and darkest tones in a print or negative.

Contrasty Negative: Negative with very dark and very light areas but almost no middle tones.

Correct Exposure: Amount of light that must strike the film in order for it to record all the tones of the image.

Cropping in the Camera: Visualizing how your photograph will look, and eliminating undesirable elements from the frame before you push the button.

Cropping in the Darkroom: Eliminating undesirable elements from the frame by racking enlarger head up to get rid of the unwanted section from the easel.

Darkroom: Light-tight room in which you process film and make prints and contact sheets.

Dense Negative: Negative that has been overexposed, and is too dark.

Depth of Field: Area in a photograph that is in sharp focus.

Diaphragm: Camera mechanism used to control the amount of light that strikes the film.

Dodging: In making an enlargement, covering one small area with a piece of cardboard or your hand in order to decrease its exposure time. Also called holding back.

Electronic Flash: Supplementary light source that is charged from either an electrical outlet or a self-contained battery pack. Also called a speedlight.

Emulsion: Chemical coating on film and printing paper that reacts with light to form a latent image.

Enlarger: Basic piece of darkroom equipment used to force light through a negative to form a positive image on printing paper.

Film Plane: Point behind the lens where the light rays meet to form a sharp image, and across which the film is stretched to record that image.

Film Speed: Time it takes for the emulsion on film to react with light to form a latent image.

Fixer: Also called hypo. Chemical that washes away unused emulsion on negatives and prints, and makes the developed image permanent.

Flashbulbs and *Flashcubes:* Camera attachments that supply a burst of supplementary light, used for shooting in low-light conditions.

Focal Length: Distance from the center of the lens to the focal plane of a camera; used in reference to the scope and range of a lens.

Focal Point: The point in back of the lens at which light rays meet and form a sharp image.

Focus: Sharpness of the image you see in the viewfinder; also, the sharpness of a print or negative.

f. Stops: Settings on a lens that determine diaphragm aperture.

Grain: The thousands of tiny dots in a photograph that make up the image.

Instamatic: Most inexpensive and easiest to operate of all cameras. Can be bought for less than $15.

Light Meter: Instrument specifically designed to "read" light and give you correct exposure information.

Light-Struck Film: Film that's been damaged by accidental exposure to light.

Negative: Exposed film on which the latent image has been developed. The tones of a negative are reversed; that is, light tones appear dark and dark tones appear light.

Negative Carrier: Part of the enlarger in which the negative is placed.

Normal Negative: Negative in which the highlight and shadow areas (dark and light) are both present, and you can see the detail in both, as well as in the middle tones.

Overexposure: Condition caused by letting too much light fall on film or printing paper.

Parallax Error: Error in composition that can happen when you're shooting with a twin-lens reflex.

Polaroid: Type of camera that processes the print in the camera itself, and delivers the print within minutes after you shoot the photograph.

Rangefinder: One kind of compact, 35 mm camera; also, the viewing system of this kind of camera.

Refraction: The property of light that causes light rays to bend when they pass through glass.

Safelight: Darkroom light that will not damage light-sensitive paper.

Shutter: Protective shield built in front of the film plane to protect the film from light.

Shutter Speed: The length of time the camera shutter is open letting light fall on the film.

SLR: Single-lens reflex camera; a compact camera with a through-the-lens viewing system.

Stopping Action: Arresting motion in a moving subject by using a fast shutter speed.

Telephoto Lens: Has a long focal length that brings faraway objects closer and magnifies them. Also called a long lens.

Test Strip: Trial print made to determine correct exposure for final print.

Thin Negative: Negative that has been underexposed and is too light.

35 millimeter: Standard film size; each frame is approximately 1½ inches wide. Also refers to cameras that take 35 mm film and to lenses with a 35 mm focal length.

Tripod: Three-legged camera support.

Twin-Lens Reflex: Camera with two lenses, one stacked above the other.

Type A Film: Color film that you use for daylight shooting.

Type B Film: Color film that you shoot in artificial, tungsten light.

Underexposure: Condition caused by letting too little light fall on film or printing paper.

Variable Contrast Paper: Printing paper whose contrast is controlled by printing with special filters.

Viewing System: Camera mechanism through which you look to see and focus the image you are going to photograph.

Wide-Angle Lens: Short focal-length lens with an angle of vision wider than that of the eye.

Further Reading

Here are some suggestions for further reading and looking. These publications were not necessarily intended for young photographers only, but for photographers of all ages.

Some of the best books I have read on photography are the titles in the Life Library of Photography, Time-Life Books, New York City. The ones that I like the most are: *The Art of Photography, Light and Film, Special Problems, The Great Themes, Photojournalism, Photographing Nature, Documentary Photography, Frontiers of Photography, Photographing Children,* and *Color.*

The Life Library publishes about two new titles a year, so keep your eyes open.

Two good monthly magazines are:
Camera 35, American Express Publishing Company, New York City
Popular Photography, Ziff-Davis Publishing Company, New York City

These are some of my favorite books of photographs:
The Concerned Photographer, and *The Concerned Photographer 2,* Grossman Publishers, New York City, 1968 and 1972. (One of the very best collections of documentary photographs from all over the world.)

John Szarkowski, ed.: *Photographs of Jacques-Henri Lartigue,* Museum of Modern Art, 1963. (In 1901, when Lartigue was seven years old, he was given his first camera by his father. Lartigue's family were inveterate inventors and daredevils, and he photographed all their mishaps with homemade airplanes,

59

parachutes, water wings, and more indescribable contraptions. This is a funny and wonderful book of photographs.)

Duane Michals: *Sequences*, Doubleday and Company, Inc., Garden City, New York, 1969. (Photographic comic strips, some funny, some mysterious, and each sequence tells a story. Can you figure out how the photographer did it?)

Garry Winogrand: *The Animals*, Museum of Modern Art, New York Graphic Society Ltd., 1969. (A new and different way of looking at the denizens of the zoo.)

Note: all of these books are available in paperback.

Index

Print developer, 46
Print-making process, 8, 46-49, 51-
    52
Prints, 8, 41, 52

Rangefinder, 7
Reel, 42, 43, 44
Refraction of light, 11
Retina, 2
Reversal, color, 33

Safelight, 46, 47, 52
Shutter, 2, 3
Shutter speeds, 17, 18, 21, 47
Silhouette effect, 29
SLR, 7, 10
Soft-contrast paper, 51
Soft-focus background, 17
Speedlight, 31
Squeegee (sponge), 42, 44
Stop bath. *See* Indicator Stop Bath

Stopping action, 18
Subject matter, 18, 21, 35, 36, 40
"Sun at back" rule, 29

Test strip, 47
Thin negative, 44, 49
35 mm cameras, 7, 8, 10
Time exposures, 21
Transparencies, 33, 34
Tripod, 18
Tungsten light, 33
Twin-lens reflex cameras, 8, 9, 10
2¼ SLR, 10

Underexposure, 26, 27, 44

Variable contrast paper, 51
Verichrome Pan (VP), 32
Viewfinder, 25
Viewing screen, 2, 3, 8, 10

ABOUT THE AUTHOR

CATHERINE NOREN is a free-lance photographer-writer based in New York City. A graduate of Bennington College, she was a high school teacher until she decided to make photography a full-time career. In addition to publication in magazines and textbooks, her work has had exhibits in New York, Minneapolis, and Milan. She is currently working on a book of photographs to be published by a major New York house in early 1974.